Searchlight BOOKS™

New Frontiers of Space

Cutting-Edge

SpaceX News

Aiyanna Milligan

Lerner Publications ◆ Minneapolis

Lerner Publications Company
An imprint of Lerner Publishing Group, Inc.
241 First Avenue North
Minneapolis, MN 55401 USA

For reading levels and more information, look up this title at www.lernerbooks.com.

Main body text set in Adrianna Regular 14/20.
Typeface provided by Chank.

Library of Congress Cataloging-in-Publication Data

Names: Milligan, Aiyanna, author.
Title: Cutting-edge SpaceX news / Aiyanna Milligan.
Description: Minneapolis : Lerner Publications, [2020] | Series: Searchlight books.
    New frontiers of space | Audience: Ages 8–11. | Audience: Grades 4 to 6. | Includes
    bibliographical references and index.
Identifiers: LCCN 2018059700 (print) | LCCN 2019004524 (ebook) | ISBN 9781541556737
    (eb pdf) | ISBN 9781541555839 (lb : alk. paper) | ISBN 9781541574878 (pb : alk. paper)
Subjects: LCSH: SpaceX (Firm)—Juvenile literature. | Space launch industry—Juvenile
    literature. | Launch vehicles (Astronautics)—Juvenile literature. | Space flight—Juvenile
    literature.
Classification: LCC TL790 (ebook) | LCC TL790 .M55 2020 (print) | DDC
    338.4/7629478—dc23

LC record available at https://lccn.loc.gov/2018059700

Manufactured in the United States of America
1-46038-43361-5/6/2019

Contents

Chapter 1

FOUNDING SPACEX

On February 6, 2018, the countdown began for the SpaceX Falcon Heavy rocket: 5, 4, 3, 2, 1. The engines fired, and flames shot down. Smoke billowed from the launch site near Cape Canaveral, Florida. Then the world's most powerful rocket launched straight up into the sky.

Falcon Heavy takes off on a test mission.

Starman sits in the Roadster with Earth in the background.

Sitting on top of the rocket was a unique payload. The rocket carried a red Tesla Roadster, an electric car. In the driver's seat was Starman, a dummy dressed in a space suit. The Roadster and its passenger are headed beyond Mars.

This Falcon Heavy test launch was a big accomplishment for SpaceX. About an hour later, two of its stages safely landed back on Earth. Another stage landed in the ocean and sank to the bottom.

Space Fact or Fiction

Starman and the Tesla Roadster have landed on Mars. That is fiction!

On November 2, 2018, the Roadster flew past Mars. The car is orbiting the sun, just as the planets in our solar system do. This path takes Starman around Mercury, Venus, Earth, and Mars. These four planets orbit closest to the sun in our solar system. The Roadster and its passenger will continue this orbit for millions of years.

Mars

ELON MUSK—ROCKET SCIENTIST, TESLA COFOUNDER, AND SPACEX FOUNDER

SpaceX is one of several private space companies. It is not a government-owned space agency. Elon Musk founded SpaceX in 2002. He is an inventor and business owner from South Africa. Musk dreamed of people living on Mars, so he started SpaceX to bring them there someday. The company designs new and improved space technology, including engines, rockets, and spacecraft.

The Costs of Space Travel

Government space agencies send astronauts and technology to space. But it costs a lot of money. A few tourists bought tickets to space on Russian spacecraft. Their tickets cost millions of dollars. That's because the Russian rockets could be used only once.

Space tourists have launched into space with the Russian Soyuz rocket.

An artist imagines the SpaceX Dragon capsule landing on Mars.

One of SpaceX's main goals is to lower the cost to go to space. So it is creating reusable rockets, boosters, and spacecraft. This saves money. With cheaper space travel, more people can visit space.

SpaceX wants to take travelers to space. One day, its rockets and spacecraft may visit distant planets and other faraway places. Maybe human colonies will spring up throughout the solar system.

Chapter 2

INSIDE SPACEX

Engineers create and test SpaceX designs in McGregor, Texas. One spacecraft is the Falcon 9. It is the world's first partly reusable rocket that can enter Earth's orbit. When Falcon 9's booster stage runs out of fuel, it detaches from the rest of the rocket. Then the booster lands safely on Earth. It can be used for future launches.

The Dragon capsule sits at the top of the Falcon 9 rocket.

Falcon Heavy's two boosters are at the sides of the rocket.

Falcon Heavy is another rocket with parts that are reusable. It has two boosters with fins and landing legs. The fins help guide the boosters back to Earth. The landing legs allow the boosters to land safely. Falcon 9 and Falcon Heavy can transport satellites and supplies into space.

Falcon rockets can carry the Dragon spacecraft. It is the only commercial spacecraft that can return to Earth and be reused. Dragon does not need a crew. The robotic spacecraft carries cargo. Once it detaches from its rocket, the Dragon capsule can fly in space. It uses solar panels and batteries for power. It has a high-tech heat shield that protects the spacecraft from temperatures up to 2,732°F (1,500°C).

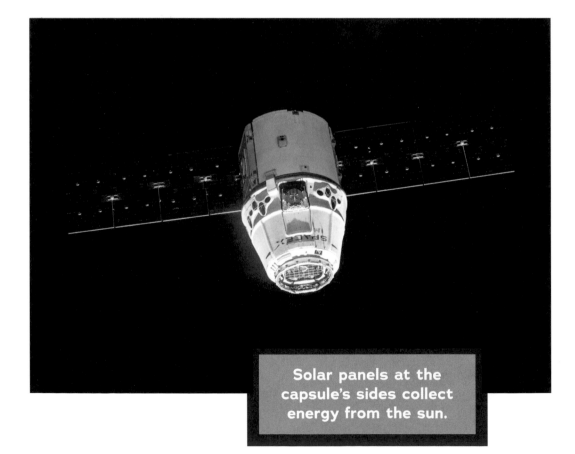

Solar panels at the capsule's sides collect energy from the sun.

Astronauts Bob Behnken (*left*) and Doug Hurley sit inside a model of a Crew Dragon spacecraft.

Dragon spacecraft will have more uses than carrying cargo. Crew Dragon will carry up to seven passengers. DragonLab will be a space laboratory. Crew can use it to perform experiments and tests.

Launch Sites

SpaceX rockets launch from three government sites. Two launch sites are in Central Florida near the Atlantic Ocean: the Kennedy Space Center and the Cape Canaveral Air Force Station, south of the space center. The third site is the Vandenberg Air Force Base, in California near the Pacific Ocean.

Falcon 9 launches from the Kennedy Space Center.

THIS SPACEX ROCKET AWAITS LAUNCH IN CALIFORNIA.

▼

SpaceX is building a fourth launch site in Boca Chica, Texas, near the Gulf of Mexico. The four sites will allow SpaceX's spacecraft to reach different parts of space. Being close to water is also good. Ships act as mobile landing pads on the water for SpaceX rocket parts.

Recovery Ships

SpaceX has two drone ships where its rockets land. A drone ship operates remotely without a crew. Each ship is almost the size of a football field! Additional vessels collect Dragon capsules and reusable rocket parts when they land in the ocean. *Mr. Steven* is a ship that acts like a safety net. The ship has four steel arms that stretch up and hold a large yellow net. Parachutes and thrusters slow rocket parts down. Then the parts safely land on the net.

Mr. Steven is designed to catch nose cones from SpaceX spacecraft.

Chapter 3

FIRST CARGO FLIGHTS

Falcon 1 was the first rocket SpaceX launched. On September 28, 2008, Falcon 1 became the first liquid-fueled rocket from a commercial company to orbit Earth.

Elon Musk (*lower left*) watches a Falcon 1 liftoff from a command center.

It achieved this feat on its fourth flight. Also in 2008, SpaceX began working with the National Aeronautics and Space Administration (NASA), the US space agency. NASA did not have rockets to send into space. So the space agency hired SpaceX to deliver cargo to the International Space Station (ISS).

NASA's Commercial Crew Program will send astronauts to space on SpaceX capsules.

A Falcon 9 launch

Falcon 9 was the next spacecraft the company made. In 2010, Falcon 9 took Dragon on its first trip. A few hours after takeoff, Dragon used braking rockets to begin its return to Earth. It splashed into the Pacific Ocean with help from parachutes. Two years later, Falcon 9 launched with Dragon again. On this flight, Dragon became the first private spacecraft to reach the ISS.

Supplying the ISS

The ISS is a space station that is also a laboratory. It orbits Earth. Space agencies from the United States, Russia, Canada, Japan, and Europe built the ISS between 1998 and 2011. Three to six astronauts from different nations take turns living aboard the station. They may stay for six months or longer. They study Earth and space. In 2016, Scott Kelly became the first American to spend 340 days there. He and Russian cosmonaut Mikhail Kornienko helped study how long space missions affect humans.

Dragon docks with the ISS to deliver cargo from Earth.

Falcon 9 hasn't just carried cargo to the ISS. On February 22, 2018, Falcon 9 brought three satellites into space. The *Paz* satellite monitors Earth and captures images for the Spanish government. Musk launched *Tintin A* and *Tintin B* satellites to test communication technology for a program called Starlink. The program's goal is to bring the internet to more people around the world.

SpaceX Failures

Not all SpaceX's launches have gone smoothly. Falcon 1 failed to launch on its first three attempts. Then, on June 28, 2015, a Falcon 9 rocket exploded during launch. The rocket was supposed to bring supplies to the ISS. SpaceX believes a faulty part caused an oxygen tank to explode. On January 17, 2016, Falcon 9 successfully launched a satellite into space. But when the rocket's booster tried to land, something went wrong. One of its landing legs failed. Then the booster tipped over and exploded. Later that year, another Falcon 9 rocket and its payload exploded.

A Falcon 9 rocket explodes shortly after takeoff in 2015.

FLIGHT DIRECTORS WATCH SPACEX LAUNCHES FROM A CONTROL CENTER.

No one has ever been hurt during a SpaceX mission. And SpaceX learned from each setback. Their failures have taught them what they need to improve. These mistakes made SpaceX change how it operates and improve vehicle designs.

Chapter 4

FUTURE CREWED MISSIONS

What's next for SpaceX? The company plans to send crewed missions to space. In 2010, NASA started the Commercial Crew Program with SpaceX and other commercial space companies. The program plans to launch astronauts to the ISS.

NASA astronaut Sunita Williams tests the technology inside a Dragon capsule.

The first NASA commercial crew is training to fly SpaceX capsules.

On August 3, 2018, NASA announced the astronauts assigned to some of these launches. Bob Behnken and Doug Hurley will test Crew Dragon in 2019. Later, Victor Glover and Mike Hopkins will fly the capsule to the ISS.

Space Tourism

SpaceX plans to bring tourists to space after testing Crew Dragon. The company already has its first passenger. Japanese business owner Yusaku Maezawa paid for a trip around the moon. He has always loved the moon and wants to see it up close. Maezawa enjoys collecting art and wants to bring some artists on the trip as part of a project called #dearMoon. After the trip, the artists will create art reflecting their experiences. The weeklong journey is planned for 2023.

Yusaku Maezawa (*center*) is the first tourist that SpaceX will bring into space.

This illustration shows what a SpaceX Mars base might look like.

Musk's first vision for SpaceX was to send humans to Mars. So the company is planning missions to the Red Planet. It plans to send supplies to Mars in 2022. Then a crewed mission would follow in 2024. The mission would deliver more cargo and set up a Mars base. Future astronauts could live at the base. They might communicate with Earth using the Deep Space Network, a system of distant satellites and three giant radio antennas on Earth. These could be the first steps toward building a city on Mars.

New Rocket Power

SpaceX is developing a new two-stage space vehicle for long spaceflights. It includes the Starship spacecraft and the Super Heavy booster rocket. Starship will be able to travel to the moon, to Mars, and in Earth's orbit. It may even speed up transportation on Earth. Trips between any two points in the world would take up to an hour.

SpaceX continues creating new, reusable space technology. The company is lowering the cost of space travel. One day, going to space may become something many people can afford. SpaceX has big plans for future space travel.

Starship may bring humans farther into space than they have ever been before.

NASA's Deep Space Network uses antennas to communicate with satellites. SpaceX may use the network on its Mars mission. The satellites are very deep in space. NASA's large antennas in California, Spain, and Australia can pick up weak signals from the distant satellites. Visit the URL below to 3D print a model of a NASA Deep Space Network antenna.

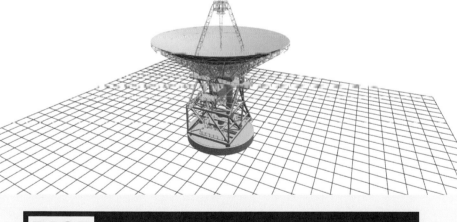

 PAGE PLUS http://qrs.lernerbooks.com/e6oe

Glossary

booster: a rocket stage that provides the initial thrust during a launch

capsule: a spacecraft designed to carry people and cargo

commercial: having to do with private businesses, not the government

orbit: an object's repeating path around a larger planet, moon, or star

payload: objects carried by a vehicle

rocket: a device that pushes out gases to accelerate spacecraft fast enough to move beyond Earth's gravity and into space

satellite: a piece of technology that orbits around Earth or another body in space

solar system: Earth and the other planets and objects orbiting our sun

stage: a section of a rocket that contains engines and fuel

thruster: a small engine on a spacecraft or rocket used to change slightly its path or speed

Learn More about SpaceX News

Books

Kruesi, Liz. *Discover Space Exploration*. Minneapolis: Lerner Publications, 2017. Find out how people study the distant stars, planets, and galaxies that make up our universe.

Kurtz, Kevin. *Cutting-Edge Space Tourism*. Minneapolis: Lerner Publications, 2020. Learn more about SpaceX and other companies that are competing to bring tourists to space.

Ventura, Marne. *Elon Musk: Entrepreneur and Innovator*. Minneapolis: Abdo, 2018. Learn about Elon Musk and his companies.

Websites

Kids News: SpaceX
https://www.kidsnews.com.au/space/spacex-successfully-launches
-worlds-most-powerful-rocket-and-sends-a-car-into-space/news
-story/e4253abdd76a49981ffdf92cdbecfe25
Learn about the first Falcon Heavy launch.

NASA for Students
https://www.nasa.gov/audience/forstudents/index.html
Select your grade group, and check out STEM resources including an edible spacecraft project and a commercial space e-book.

National Geographic Kids: Passport to Space
https://kids.nationalgeographic.com/explore/space/passport
-to-space/
View photos, play games, take quizzes, and more as you experience all things space.

Index

Photo Acknowledgments

Image credits: courtesy of SpaceX, pp. 4, 5, 9, 11, 14, 15, 18, 24, 27, 28; NASA/JPL/MSSS, p. 6; Paul Harris/Getty Images, p. 7; NASA/Joel Kowsky, pp. 8, 10; NASA, pp. 12, 13, 20, 23; ZUMA Press, Inc/Alamy Stock Photo, p. 16; Axel Koester/Corbis/Getty Images, p. 17; Chris Thompson/SpaceX, p. 19; courtesy AIRBUS SAS, p.21; Red Huber/Orlando Sentinel/TNS/Getty Images, p. 22; NASA/Robert Markowitz, p. 25; The Asahi Shimbun/Getty Images, p. 26; Brian Kumanchik, Christian Lopez. NASA/JPL-Caltech, p. 29 (image and project).

Cover: courtesy of SpaceX.